VEGAN Anniversary in the Bay Area

A Decade of Sweet Memories from Brazil and Cultural Exchanges in the United States

Written by Thaisa Fernandes | Photos by Izabelle Alvares

BEYOND BORDERS PUBLISHING

To my
immigrant
friends

2024 is a significant milestone for me. I've spent a decade living in San Francisco, practicing yoga, veganism, and finding myself. These past 10 years have been a journey. It's fascinating to see how embracing new habits and experiences in 2014 shaped my personal evolution.

Living abroad brought challenges and new experiences. A decade ago, I embarked on a path that allowed me to explore what truly makes me happy, free from others' expectations. I had just moved to a new country and, at the same time, decided to go vegan after being vegetarian for a year.

As I write this, I've just finalized the book and reviewed the recipes. It's incredibly fulfilling to see years of work and countless recipe tests come together. Writing this book has been a decade-long endeavor that I'm immensely proud of.

If you're wondering why I moved to the United States, my answer aligns with that of many other Latin and Caribbean immigrants: for the hope of a better life.

As for why I became vegan, it's about animal rights. I believe every creature deserves life. I don't think humans are more important than animals, nor should we prioritize our lives over theirs.

Coming from Minas Gerais, Brazil—a region known for its meat and dairy-heavy cuisine—I often joke that

Minas and Bahia have the best food in Brazil, blending African and Portuguese influences. I grew up around *churrasco* (barbecue) culture and loved to eat meat, especially beef and cheese. So no, I didn't stop eating meat and dairy because I didn't like them, but I don't think my taste should outweigh an animal's life.

The recipes in this book are all vegan, surprise! At the same time, I'm not here to convince you to go vegan or judge your food choices. I would like to invite you to try new recipes and cuisines. Many of the dishes you're going to find in this book are Brazilian with influences from my cultural background. You'll find classics like cheese bread (*pão de queijo*), carrot cake, guava (*goiabinha*) cookies, flan (*pudim*), and also American and French favorites like cookies, sweet potato pie, crème brûlée and croissant.

The ingredients used in this book are simple—flour, non-dairy milk, sugar, and dark chocolate. You don't need any fancy tools or ingredients. All the recipes can be made by hand, with no need for a mixer or blender (though feel free to use them if you have them).

Recently, I was excited to find vegan oat condensed milk, which brought back memories of traditional recipes I loved. It made me reflect on how much veganism has evolved in the past 10 years. Non-dairy milk and vegan products are now easy to find, even in rural U.S. areas. In Brazil, cities like Belo Horizonte and São Paulo have become increasingly vegan-friendly. I'm also always grateful when I return home and can find rice, beans, fried bananas, salad, *acarajé, açaí,* and many amazing tropical fruits wherever I go.

Even if you're not much of a cook, I encourage you to read the stories and enjoy the process. We'll share behind-the-scenes moments and cool food illustrations. Perhaps you can even consider helping a friend pre-

pare a recipe or simply displaying this beautiful book in your living room.

As someone who loves books but isn't attached to them, I encourage you to re-gift this book to a friend after reading it if you feel inspired. After all, "sharing is caring", isn't that what they say?

Sinta-se em casa. I hope you feel welcomed.
Thaisa Fernandes

Pão De Queijo (Cheese Bread)	8
Brazilian Carrot Cake	12
Goiabinha (Guava Cookie)	16
Pudim (Brazilian Flan)	21
Brigadeiro (Chocolate Truffle)	24
Pistachio & Chocolate Cookie	28
Vanilla Cake	32
Sweet Potato Pie	36
Creme Brulée	40
Croissant	44
Bonus: Blueberry Dog Muffins!	50

I'm from a state in Brazil called Minas Gerais. Unlike the typical image of Brazil with its beaches, in my state, we're surrounded by beautiful mountains. I might be a bit biased, but I believe my region boasts the best food and Carnival parties, with a culinary heritage that blends indigenous, African, and Portuguese influences.

One of the most famous Brazilian snacks is *"pão de queijo,"* or cheese bread, or cheese puffs. I love hearing people try to pronounce it! I joke that I can recognize a good, authentic *pão de queijo* just by looking at it—the shape, color, and overall vibe are crucial to me. When I turned vegan, one of the first recipes I attempted to veganize was *pão de queijo*.

Enjoying *pão de queijo* evokes incredible moments with loved ones—drinking coffee, chatting, and sharing stories. Every time I return to my hometown, my mom, Sayonara, sets the table with a crochet or cross-stitch tablecloth made by our family and brews coffee while we wait for the vegan *pão de queijo* to be baked.

Living as an immigrant can sometimes feel lonely. I often reflect on how challenging it is to navigate someone else's culture. These reflections deepen my appreciation for the time spent with family. I truly value the effort someone puts into cooking for me, especially with limited options (hello, vegan friends), and I cherish those moments we share even more now.

Living as an immigrant can sometimes feel lonely. I often reflect on how challenging it is to navigate someone else's culture.

PÃO DE QUEIJO (CHEESE BREAD)

Serving

About 40 medium-sized balls

Timing

Bake for 35-40 minutes at 400°F (204°C)

Gluten Free

Nut Free

Ingredients

- 1 and ½ cups (315 g) cooked and mashed potatoes
- ⅓ cup (24 g) nutritional yeast
- 1 teaspoon salt
- ¼ cup (60 ml) vegetable oil
- ½ cup (120 ml) hot water
- ½ cup (120 g) shredded non-dairy cheese
- 2 cups (240 g) tapioca flour
- Optional: Add ⅓ cup (40 g) vegan bacon bits if you're feeling sassy

Preparation

- **Preheat the oven** to 400°F (204°C)
- **Cook and mash** the potato, then add it to a bowl
- **Add** the nutritional yeast and salt, and mix well
- **Incorporate** the vegetable oil and mix again
- **Pour in** the hot water and mix until combined
- **Add** the shredded non-dairy cheese and the flour(s)
- **Mix everything** until you get a homogeneous dough
- **Optional:** Add the vegan bacon bits
- **Roll small portions** into medium-sized balls

Finishing

- **Line a baking sheet** with parchment paper or a Silpat
- **Arrange** the *pão de queijo* balls on the sheet, leaving some space between them
- **If you're not baking all of them at once**, store the remaining in a container that fits in your freezer

Extra points if you visit a Brazilian market, use 1 and ½ cups (315 g) sour manioc starch (polvilho azedo) + ½ cup (120 g) tapioca flour instead

Birthday parties filled with joy and excitement are amongst my favorite childhood memories. The table with a lot of sweets — *brigadeiro, cajuzinho, beijinho, olho de sogra, and moranguinho*—sparkled with sugar and promise.

Bala de coco nestled in colorful wrappers, and of course those iconic small soda glass bottles, adding to the festive atmosphere. Hats and plushies were scattered around, and the table brimmed with candles waiting to be lit.

Kids eagerly awaited the countdown, their eyes gleaming with anticipation. The rule was clear: no one could touch the treats until after the birthday song. This tradition created a sense of suspense as we all gathered around the cake, ready to sing our hearts out. While the parties usually featured a chocolate cake, I always wished for a Brazilian carrot cake, one of my favorites.

It was essential to clap while singing the birthday song, a funny difference to how celebrations were done in the United States, where people clap only at the end. Reflecting on those moments, I realize how much my aunt, Élida, my grandmother, Iolanda, and my godmother, Neuza, influenced my love for sweets. My grandma, Ana Carmen, used to make a lot of naturally vegan sweets, of course, I had no idea about it at that time but her papaya and fig sweets were the best. All those amazing women showed me the magic of creating something wonderful with your own hands, transforming simple ingredients into delightful treats that brought happiness to everyone.

Growing up struggling financially made these parties even more special. They felt like a rare and precious event, an almost once-in-a-lifetime experience of candy overload. Each party was a treasured memory. These experiences instilled in me a deep appreciation for the art of baking and the joy of sharing sweets, shaping my love for creating and enjoying these little moments of happiness.

BRAZILIAN CARROT CAKE

Serving

8-inch (20 cm) cake

Timing

Bake for 35-40 minutes at 400°F (200°C)

Ingredients

CAKE

- 2 cups (250 g) raw sliced carrots
- ¾ cup (160 g) sugar
- ½ cup vegetable oil
- 1 cup (240 ml) room temperature water
- 2 cups (250 g) all-purpose flour, sifted
- ¼ teaspoon salt
- 1 teaspoon baking powder
- 1 teaspoon vinegar

CHOCOLATE COVER

- 60 g dark chocolate
- 4 teaspoons non-dairy milk

Preparation

- **Preheat the oven** to 400°F (200°C)
- **In a blender,** combine the sliced carrots
- **Blend for at least 3 minutes** to break down the carrot fibers
- **Set a timer** to ensure thorough blending
- **If you don't have a blender,** cut the carrots into smaller pieces as much as you can
- **Gently mix** the sugar, vegetable oil, and water into the carrot mixture
- **In a large mixing bowl,** sift together the all-purpose flour and salt
- **Add the baking powder** and mix gently
- **Pour the carrot mixture** into the bowl with the dry ingredients
- **Add the vinegar** and mix until just combined
- **Be careful** not to overmix
- **Pour the batter** into the cake pan

Mix the dough carefully and make sure not to overmix it. Avoid opening the oven for at least the first 20 minutes to ensure proper rising of the cake

The rule was clear: no one could touch the treats until after the birthday song.

Eating a whole bag of *goiabinha* cookies often feels like a temporary escape from reality, a quick fix for a bad day. Who hasn't been there? That instant gratification eases anxiety, even if only for a few minutes, before the sugar crash brings it back in full force.

I've always struggled with balance. Sometimes, the need for comfort runs deeper than the fleeting joy of finishing a bag of treats—and that's okay. Anxiety often pushes us into these patterns of compulsion, and it took me years to understand that connection. Eating can become automatic, a way to fill an emotional void.

It's so sad to see how fatphobic our society is. Depending on your body type, these compulsions can either be dismissed or harshly judged. It's important to acknowledge that it's okay to indulge in a whole bag of sweets. With all the conflicts and political challenges in the world, just living our lives is hard enough—so why should we feel guilty about eating cookies?

My partner, Koji, reminded me of a special kind of store we have in our state in Brazil called *Loja de Biscoito*—the homemade cookie shop. In Brazil, vegan *goiabinha* is rare, even in homemade cookie stores, though it's surprisingly easy to veganize. Like many Brazilians, it's impossible to control myself when I have *goiabinhas* around me. On the other hand, understanding the balance between indulgence and mindful eating allows me to truly savor food. I'm thrilled to know I can enjoy *goiabinha* cookies again as a vegan!

With all the conflicts and political challenges in the world, just living our lives is hard enough—so why should we feel guilty about eating cookies?

GOIABINHA (GUAVA COOKIE)

Gluten Free

Nut Free

Serving

Makes around 80 guava cookies

Timing

Bake for 15-25 minutes at 350°F (180°C)

Ingredients

- 4 cups (500 g) cornstarch
- 1 cup (200 g) butter
- 1 cup (300 g) oat or coconut condensed milk
- Guava sweets or guava paste found at Brazilian or Latin markets

Modeling

- **Preheat the oven** to 350°F (180°C)
- **Roll the dough** into small, evenly sized balls
- **Use your fingertip** to create a cavity in the center of each ball
- **Fill the cavity** with a small amount of guava sweet or guava paste
- **Let them rest** in the refrigerator for 15 minutes

Preparation

- **Mix the cornstarch** with butter until it reaches a sandy consistency
- **Slowly add** the condensed milk, mixing until well combined
- **Wrap the dough** in plastic wrap and refrigerate it for 15-30 minutes

Finishing

- **Line a baking sheet** with parchment paper or a Silpat
- **Arrange the guava cookies** on the sheet, leaving space between them

Avoid over-browning to maintain their melt-in-the-mouth texture

Allow the guava cookies to cool completely on a rack before serving

If you prefer or can't find the Brazilian guava sweet, you can make this recipe without them, turning it into another type of cookie called *sequilho* or *biscoito quebra-quebra*

I love to cook and believe it's an essential skill everyone should have. Unfortunately, many people view it as a "gift" only women possess and should perform at all costs. How can a fundamental human survival skill like cooking not be cherished and practiced by everyone?

Pudim, the Brazilian flan, is a rich Portuguese dessert made with condensed milk and egg yolks. Its roots trace back to the 19th century. Since turning vegan, I've started to veganize my favorite dishes. One of the most challenging was *pudim*; it was probably the last dish I managed to recreate. I even made vegan meringue and macaroons before mastering *pudim*.

In researching the history of pudim, I discovered that the word "flan" comes from the Latin word *"fladon"*, which originates from the Old High German word *"flado"*, meaning flat cake. One of the first Roman versions of flan was made with eel sprinkled with pepper—sounds extremely gross. The Spaniards brought it to the American continent, where it became a delicacy. Due to Mexican influence *(gracias, familia)*, the recipe evolved into today's sweet staple—a delightful transformation, in my opinion.

Flan is a popular and beloved dessert in many Spanish-speaking countries, as well as in Brazil and the Philippines, a legacy of colonization. It was also a dessert my mom loved to make. From a young age, I took on the responsibility of baking, eagerly accepting the task, but I never attempted to make a *pudim* since my mom's was always the best. When I created this recipe, many friends were excited to sample my experiments, and their joy in trying it was truly amazing. I love how food can evoke cherished memories. I hope you enjoy this recipe; it is extra special to me!

One of the first Roman versions of flan was made with eel sprinkled with pepper—sounds extremely gross. The Spaniards brought it to the American continent, where it became a delicacy.

PUDIM (BRAZILIAN FLAN)

Gluten Free

Nut Free

Serving

Small or medium flan or cake pan

Timing

3 hours to prepare, including the fridge time

Ingredients

CARAMEL

- ½ cup (100 g) sugar

PUDIM

- 2 cans (1 and ¼ cups or 300 ml) soy cream or coconut cream
- ½ teaspoon agar agar
- Optional: Pinch of ground Kala Namak (black salt)
- ¼ cup (60 ml) maple syrup
- 2 tablespoons (30 ml) vanilla extract

Preparation

CARAMEL

- **Pour** ½ cup (120 ml) maple syrup into a pan
- **On medium-high heat**, wait for the sugar to melt
- **Wait until** it's completely melted
- **Pour the caramel** into the pudding tin where the flan will set, and set it aside

PUDIM

- **In a pan**, combine the soy cream or coconut cream and agar agar
- **Optional**: Add a pinch of ground kala namak
- **Add** ¼ cup (60 ml) of maple syrup
- **Mix in the vanilla extract** until all ingredients are combined
- **Bring the mixture to a boil** while stirring constantly
- **Pour the mixture** into a pudding tin (small or medium), where the caramel is, distributing it evenly
- **Place the tin in the fridge** for 2 hours to set
- **Remove the flan** from the tin just before serving

If you can't find coconut cream, you can use canned coconut milk instead, adding an extra pinch of agar-agar

Brigadeiro brings me countless memories.
In our typical Latin American family, food is a
centerpiece—making sure everyone is well-fed
is non-negotiable. You'd better clean your plate
or have a convincing excuse, though it'll likely be
overlooked. Some of my best childhood memories
are around birthday parties with family and friends.

Like many kids in Latin America during the 90s and 2000s, our celebrations were filled with sweets, cookies, cake, and soda. My grandma, Iolanda, always made the best *brigadeiros* for these occasions, and surprisingly, they tasted even better after a few days—a delightful surprise!

Brigadeiro, a sweet made from condensed milk, butter, and chocolate, is a staple at Brazilian birthday parties and celebrations. I believe adults should celebrate their birthdays as we did when we were kids—with balloons, cake, and any other decorations you like. It doesn't matter if you have kids or not; I grant you permission to celebrate your birthdays like you did when you were younger. Use this book to prove that your permission was granted!

As we repeatedly lose our reproductive rights, I am reminded of how society is diminishing access to abortion and how compulsory maternity persists. The challenges of becoming a mother or parent seem to grow over the years. Even deciding to be a dog or cat mom feels daunting in this patriarchal and capitalist society, where nothing is ever enough and women are often seen as inadequate. Celebrating silly moments like birthdays can feel like a luxury when we are grappling with so many important issues. At the same time, I believe it becomes even more important to celebrate significant moments with loved ones because of that.

BRIGADEIRO (CHOCOLATE TRUFFLE)

Serving

Makes 40 medium size balls

Timing

15-30 minutes to prepare

Ingredients

- 1 cup (240 g) oat condensed milk
- 1 and ½ (480 g) coconut milk powder
- ½ cup (125 g) coconut sugar
- 5 tablespoons (40 g) cocoa powder
- 2 teaspoons filtered water
- 1 teaspoon (5 g) vegan butter
- Optional: Chocolate sprinkles

Preparation

- **Combine the condensed milk** with the coconut milk powder in a pan
- **On medium-low heat**, add the coconut sugar and cocoa powder
- **Add the water** and keep mixing it
- **Keep mixing it,** don't let it boil; reduce the temperature if needed
- **Cook and stir** until thickened, about 10 minutes
- **Remove from heat** and let rest until the mixture is cool enough to handle
- **Place it in the fridge** for at least 30 minutes to firm it up
- **Roll small portions** into medium-sized balls
- **Optional:** Coat in sprinkles

Place the dough in the fridge for at least 30 minutes to firm up before rolling the balls

The challenges of becoming a mother or parent seem to grow over the years. Even deciding to be a dog or cat mom feels daunting in this patriarchal and capitalist society, where nothing is ever enough and women are often seen as inadequate.

I moved to the United States in 2014, always eager to try authentic American cookies—the kind we see in the movies. In Brazil, we have American cookies, but they typically come boxed and always seemed boring to me. The influence of North American pop culture significantly shaped my expectations and desires, as it does for many of us.

Upon moving to San Francisco, I was excited to discover that vegan cookies were available in many places. I tried a bunch of them, perhaps hoping to replicate the joy I saw on screen. During the pandemic, I began experimenting with different cookie recipes in search of the perfect one.

Living in the United States for the past ten years has gradually molded my taste. Exposure to this new culture has shifted my taste and preferences whether I like it or not—though that could be a topic for another book. I learned that there are seven different kinds of cookies: drop cookies, rolled or cutout cookies, sandwich cookies, filled cookies, cookie bars, molded cookies, no-bake cookies, and pressed cookies. Drop cookies are the ones I usually bake.

Baking cookies made me happy during the challenging times of the pandemic. Each recipe instilled hope in me, and perhaps that's what baking cookies is all about—a way to affirm that everything will be fine, at least until we have cookies (and movies). Baking cookies helped me uncover other parts of myself and connect with the feelings I had always sought when looking at those images on screen.

Exposure to North American culture has shifted my taste and preferences whether I like it or not—though that could be a topic for another book.

PISTACHIO + CHOCOLATE COOKIE

Serving

Makes about 28 medium-sized cookies

Timing

Bake for 20 minutes at 350°F (180°C)

Ingredients

- 1 tablespoon ground flaxseeds
- 3 tablespoons water
- ½ cup (120 g) butter, slightly softened to room temperature
- 1 and ¼ cups (250 g) brown sugar, lightly packed
- 2 teaspoons vanilla extract
- 1 and ½ cups (180 g) all-purpose flour
- 2 teaspoons cornstarch
- 1 teaspoon baking soda
- ¼ teaspoon salt
- ½ cup (120 g) chocolate chips
- ½ cup (120 g) pistachios
- Optional: A pinch of salt flakes after baking

This cookie can be nut free if you remove the pistachios

Preparation

VEGAN EGG

- **Mix the ground flaxseed** and water in a small bowl to make the flax egg
- **Set aside**

COOKIE DOUGH

- **In a mixing bowl,** beat the softened butter and brown sugar by hand or with a mixer for 1–2 minutes until creamy
- **Add the vanilla extract** and the flax egg, mixing until combined
- **Add the flour,** cornstarch, baking soda, and salt. Mix until just combined
- **Fold in** the chocolate chips and pistachios until evenly distributed
- **Ensure** the dough is homogeneous
- **Roll small portions** into medium-sized balls

Finishing

- **Line a baking sheet** with parchment paper or a Silpat
- **Arrange** the cookie dough balls on the sheet, leaving some space between each
- **Optional**: Sprinkle salt flakes over the cookies after baking for extra awesomeness!

Each recipe brought me hope, and maybe that's what baking cookies is all about.

It's interesting when people use the term "vanilla" to describe someone. In Portuguese, we don't have an equivalent term; perhaps because we add condensed milk to everything rather than vanilla. Vanilla cakes, however, are a fail-safe choice—always delightful.

This makes me reflect on the power of cakes. When I lost my 18-year-old cat, my neighbor, in a thoughtful gesture, baked me a cake. It was a specific Brazilian cake known as "*broa de fubá*", or corn cake. Her effort to make something so special during a difficult time touched me deeply.

Cakes, in many ways, embody our connections. My maternal family are Holocaust survivors, and I resonate with Esther Perel's observation that there are two types of families—those who discuss the past and those who don't. My family is the latter. I truly believe in the importance of sharing feelings and perspectives, though I know it's not always easy or safe for everyone to do so.

In solidarity with my beliefs against the genocide happening in Gaza, I displayed a Palestinian flag in my window. One day, a neighbor expressed her gratitude and later surprised me with a vegan cake she had baked. This unexpected gesture reminded me once again of the simple yet powerful way baking connects us—whether with friends, family, neighbors, or even those we want to support.

There are two types of families—those who discuss the past and those who don't. My family is the latter.

VANILLA CAKE

Serving

Makes one 8-inch (20cm) cake

Timing

Bake for 35-40 minutes at 350°F (180°C)

Ingredients

CAKE

- 1 cup (240 ml) non-dairy milk
- 1 tablespoon vinegar
- 1 and ½ cups (180 g) all-purpose flour
- ¾ cup (150 g) granulated sugar
- 2 teaspoons baking powder
- ½ teaspoon baking soda
- ¼ teaspoon salt
- ⅓ cup (80 ml) vegetable oil
- 1 tablespoon vanilla extract
- Optional: Colorful sprinkles

FROSTING

- ½ cup (120 g) vegan butter, softened
- 2 cups (250 g) powdered sugar, sifted
- 1 teaspoon vanilla extract
- 1 teaspoon non-dairy milk

Avoid opening the oven for at least the first 20 minutes to ensure proper rising of the cake

Preparation

CAKE

- **Preheat** the oven to 350°F (180°C)
- **In a bowl, combine** the non-dairy milk and vinegar. Set aside to curdle for 5 minutes
- **In a separate bowl, whisk** together the flour, sugar, baking powder, baking soda, and salt
- **Make a well** in the center of the dry ingredients
- **Add the oil**, vanilla extract, and the milk-vinegar mixture to the well
- **Whisk** until just combined
- **Optional:** Fold in colorful sprinkles
- **Pour the batter** into a greased 8-inch (20 cm) cake pan

FROSTING

- **In a large mixing bowl, add** the vegan butter
- **Use an electric mixer** on low speed for 30 seconds until soft and creamy
- **Use your hands to mix** the ingredients in the bowl if you prefer a more hands-on approach
- **Gradually add** the powdered sugar and vanilla extract, beating until a soft frosting forms
- **If the frosting is too thick**, add a touch of non-dairy milk
- **If it's too soft**, place it in the fridge to firm up
- **Use a spatula to frost** the top of the cooled cake
- **Optional:** Decorate with sprinkles

I've always been fascinated by American culinary traditions and their deep appreciation for pies. Pies symbolize warmth, comfort, and tradition, making them a cultural icon. Veganizing a classic like sweet potato pie felt like a challenge worth pursuing—a way to honor tradition while making it vegan accessible.

Sweet potato pie holds a significant place in the Southern states, where sweet potatoes thrive. Its origins resonate with the cuisine of my home state, Minas Gerais, steeped in African diaspora influences and rich hospitality. This connection embodies the region's love for hearty meals and communal dining experiences I cherish.

Reflecting on sweet potato pie, I think of its role at family gatherings and special occasions. Every year, my closest friends, Navneet and Rohan, along with my partner, Koji, and I celebrate Friendsgiving. We blend Brazilian, Indian, Japanese, and American dishes that honor our diverse heritages and shared experiences in our adopted country, the United States.

This tradition has given Thanksgiving new meaning for me, a holiday unfamiliar in my culture. It has become a time when I deeply appreciate and celebrate my friendships, while embracing new culinary delights like biscuits and gravy, the Beef Wellington that Koji makes, which has become a must at these celebrations, Navneet's momos that I'm always so excited about, tikka masala, tofu, and, of course, sweet potato pie that we've learned to love.

Veganizing a classic like sweet potato pie felt like a challenge worth pursuing—a way to honor tradition while making it vegan accessible.

SWEET POTATO PIE

Serving

8 pie slices

Timing

Bake for 55-60 minutes at 350°F (180°C)

Ingredients

PIE CRUST

- 1 and ½ cups (188 g) all-purpose flour
- 1 teaspoon sugar
- ¼ teaspoon salt
- ¼ cup (57 g) vegan butter, cold
- ¼ cup (57 g) coconut oil, the colder the better
- 3 tablespoons ice water

SWEET POTATO FILLING

- 1 pound (454 g) or about 2 medium sweet potatoes
- ¾ cup (177 ml) coconut milk
- 1 cup (220 g) brown sugar
- 1 teaspoon vanilla extract
- 1 teaspoon ground cinnamon
- ½ cup (120 ml) orange juice
- ¼ teaspoon ground ginger
- ½ teaspoon ground nutmeg
- ¼ teaspoon salt
- 4 tablespoons (30 g) cornstarch
- Optional: Vegan whipped cream

Preparation

PIE CRUST

- **Make sure** your vegan butter and coconut oil are very cold before starting
- **If not, refrigerate them** for at least 30 minutes
- **Add flour**, sugar, and salt to the food processor fitted with the "S" blade
- **Add the cold vegan butter** and coconut oil
- **Process for about 10 seconds**, until it resembles coarse meal
- **With the food processor running**, drizzle in 3 tablespoons of ice-cold water
- **When it begins to clump together**, stop
- **You may need to add** 1 more tablespoon of ice water for it to come together
- **If you don't have a food processor,** follow the same steps manually
- **Dump the dough** onto a lightly floured surface and shape it into a ball
- **Avoid using your hands too much** to prevent warming the dough
- **If the dough is warm**, it can make your pie crust less flaky
- **Roll the dough** with a rolling pin to about a 12-inch (30 cm) circle
- **Gently lift it** using a rolling pin and carefully transfer it to a pie plate
- **Press the pie crust** gently all around the dish
- **Trim off any excess** and repair any spots as needed
- **It's now ready to use** immediately or refrigerate until you're ready to use it

SWEET POTATO FILLING

- **Keep the Vegan Pie Crust in the refrigerator** while you prepare the filling

- **Preheat the oven** to 350°F (180°C)

- **Peel and chop** the sweet potatoes

- **Place the potatoes** in a medium saucepan and add enough water to cover

- **Bring to a boil**, then reduce the heat and simmer for 12-15 minutes until fork-tender

- **Drain the potatoes** and add them to a large bowl or a stand mixer

- **Using a mixer, beat** the potatoes until smooth

- **If you don't have a mixer,** follow the same steps manually

- **Add all the remaining ingredients**, except the whipped cream

- **Beat on high speed** until smooth and well combined

- **Spread the sweet potato** filling evenly into the prepared pie crust

- **Bake for 55-60 minutes**, until the center is only slightly jiggly

- **If the crust begins to brown too much**, use a pie shield or cover the edges with aluminum foil for the last half of baking

- **Allow the pie to cool** on a cooling rack for about an hour before slicing and serving

- **Optional:** Serve with vegan whipped cream, if desired

If you don't have a blender or food processor, use your hands instead!

The feeling of breaking caramel has always fascinated me—I've wanted to experience it for as long as I can remember. Despite never having had a non-vegan crème brûlée, I was bold enough to create my own recipe. You might wonder, how did I make a recipe for something I've never tasted? I tested it with honest friends who had tried the "real" dessert.

It's interesting how we form ideas about things based on others' descriptions. I'll never know how a non-vegan crème brûlée actually tastes; I've never liked eggs, and their smell makes me feel nauseous. I also have a complicated relationship with kala namak, the sulfurous salt, because of its strong eggy odor.

This reflection reminds me of the importance of empathy. While we may never fully understand another person's experiences—whether they involve microaggressions, ableism, racism, homophobia, sexism, or countless other injustices—we can still foster empathy. Listening to people from different backgrounds helps us better understand and become more compassionate toward their journeys.

Breaking caramel symbolizes the joy of transformation—the idea that sometimes things need to break for something better to emerge. Often, things must end or be broken before the hidden treasures within can be revealed. It's a reminder to find your creative outlet—whether it's writing, art, or another form of expression—and to prioritize listening to others with different perspectives.

CRÈME BRULÉE

Serving

Makes 6 ramekins (6 oz or 180 ml)

Timing

Refrigerate for at least 2 hours before serving to allow it to firm up

Ingredients

CHOCOLATE MOUSSE

· ½ cup (120 ml) non-dairy milk

· 1 and ½ cups (225 g) dark chocolate

CRÈME

· 2 cans (1 and ¼ cups or 300 ml) coconut cream

· ½ teaspoon agar agar

· 2 tablespoons vanilla extract

· ½ cup (120 ml) maple syrup

· Optional: A pinch of ground Kala Namak (black salt) and 2 pinches of turmeric for coloring

CARAMEL

· 1 tablespoon sugar

· Torch to make the caramel

If you don't have a torch, you can use your oven broiler until the sugar melts completely. Alternatively, you can use a lighter (though it's slower, it works!)

Preparation

CHOCOLATE MOUSSE

· **Into a pan pour** the non-dairy milk

· **Add** the dark chocolate

· **Wait until the chocolate melts** and fully combines with the milk

· **Pour a small amount** into the bottom of each ramekin

· **Place in the fridge** for 1 hour

· **Or place it** for a few minutes in the freezer to speed up the process

CRÈME

· **In a pan add** the cans of coconut cream

· **Dissolve the agar agar** in a small portion of the coconut cream, mixing well

· **Combine the agar agar** mixture with the rest of the coconut cream in the pan

· **Add the vanilla extract** and maple syrup

· **Bring the crème** into a gentle boil

· **Optional:** Add Kala Namak and turmeric if desired

· **Pour the crème** into the ramekins with the chocolate mousse

· **Chill in the fridge** for at least 2 hours to set

CARAMEL

· **Take the ramekins** out of the fridge

· **Add a tablespoon of sugar** to the top of each ramekin

· **Use a torch** to melt the sugar quickly or use your oven broiler option or a lighter

Breaking caramel symbolizes the joy of transformation—the idea that sometimes things need to break for something better to emerge.

Making vegan croissants is a true challenge. If baking traditional croissants is a level 10 difficulty, then vegan croissants are a level 25. But I love challenges. I've always adored croissants and wanted to replicate the technique of making traditional ones. Selfishly, I also wanted to prove that vegan baking can rival classic methods (sorry, not sorry).

When I reflect on manual labor, I think about my family and how they inspired me. As a kid, I used to visit my father's friend's house, and they had a blackberry tree and made jam with the berries. That experience truly inspired me and made me realize how amazing it is to create things with your own hands.

Baking has taught me many valuable lessons: patience, perseverance, time management, and love. Each step—from mixing the dough to folding in the butter—demands careful attention and affection. Special thanks to Miyoko Schinner for the vegan butter awesomeness!

Croissants cannot be rushed. I remember my old self trying to expedite the process of baking croissants in two days instead of three. In a society that often undervalues manual work, the meticulous and labor-intensive process of making croissants serves as a reminder of the beauty and satisfaction that come from artisanal skills—something we need to consciously appreciate and compensate for, especially in today's world.

Baking has taught me many valuable lessons: patience, perseverance, time management, and love.

Croissants can be intimidating to make. I've baked them many times, and I always feel nervous. I'm forever thankful for the vegan chefs and everyday home cooks who are courageous enough to share their recipes. One of these special people is Mary Lin from Mary's Test Kitchen, who created the recipe I'm going to share with you. Thank you, Mary, you're incredible! Check her website: **www.marystestkitchen.com**

CROISSANT

Serving

12 croissants

Timing

Prep time: 3 days | Cooking time: 35 minutes

400°F (205°C) for ten minutes | 350°F (177°C) for 20-25 minutes

Ingredients

CROISSANT DOUGH

- 4 cups (500 g) all-purpose flour
- 1 envelope or 2 and ¼ tsp (7 g) instant yeast
- ¼ cup (60 g) sugar
- 12 g salt (2 tsp)
- ½ cup + 1 tbsp + 1 tsp (140 ml) cold water
- ½ cup + 1 tbsp + 1 tsp (140 ml) cold plant-based milk
- 3 tbs (45 g) vegan butter, softened at room temperature

VEGAN BUTTER SQUARE

- 2 sticks (227 g) vegan butter, very cold

SYRUP WASH

- 2 tablespoons maple syrup
- 4 tablespoons water

Preparation

DAY 1
MAKE THE CROISSANT DOUGH

- **In a large mixing bowl combine** flour, instant yeast, sugar, and salt
- **Use your stand mixer** or just your hands
- **Mix in** the cold plant-based milk, water and vegan butter
- **Roll it** into a square shape about 10.25" (26 cm) on each side
- **Wrap and refrigerate it**

MAKE THE BUTTER SQUARE

- **Prepare a piece of parchment paper** or wax paper by folding the edges in so that the creases form a 7.5" (19 cm) square in the middle
- **Make sure** there is enough material around the sides to completely envelop the middle
- **Slice up** the sticks of vegan butter lengthwise to make 4 to 6 slabs
- **Unfold the paper** and place the butter in the middle
- **Fold up the sides** and flip so the ends are tucked under
- **Use a rolling pin** to flatten the butter
- **Press down the butter** with the rolling pin so that the butter spreads to the edges of the paper
- **Use enough force** to spread the butter but not so much that you rip the paper
- **When the butter is evenly spread** to form a square, refrigerate

REFRIGERATE

- **Refrigerate both** the dough and butter squares for 12 to 24 hours

DAY 2
LAMINATE

- **Unwrap your vegan butter** square and place it with the angles pointed to the halfway points of each edge of the dough

- **Fold the corners of the dough** snugly over the edges of the butter, bringing the points to meet over the center of the butter

- **Press and seal the edges together** so that the vegan butter is completely enveloped by dough

- **Flatten the dough square** and the vegan butter evenly by straight press down with your floured rolling pin across the center of the dough and repeat up and down to lengthen the square into a rectangle

- **If it springs back** that means the gluten has tightened and you should wrap it back up and send it to the fridge to relax for a half hour or so before continuing

- **Roll in one direction** to gently lengthen the dough without breaking through to the vegan butter layer

- **Pat the sides** in to keep them straight

- **Aim for dimensions** of 8" x 24" (24 cm x 60 cm)

- **Sprinkle flour** as needed to prevent sticking

- **Dust off excess** flour before folding

- **Fold one end** about ⅔ of the way to the other side and fold the other end in so that the two ends meet

- **Nudge the edges together** without pulling or pressing too much

- **Don't create weak spots** which will tear the dough and reveal the butter inside

- **Fold the top down again,** this time all the way to the new bottom edge. Just in half like a book. Now there are four layers of butter

- **Wrap dough in parchment** so it can relax and the butter can firm up again in the fridge for at least a half hour. Optional, add it to a freezer bag

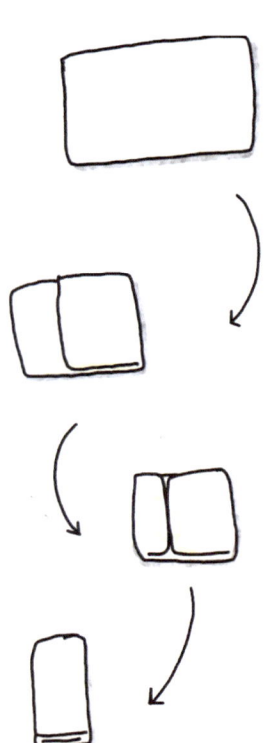

SECOND AND THIRD TURNS

- **Place the dough down** so a short end is facing you

- **Flatten the dough** like before, pressing straight down across the width, up and down the length

- **Roll the dough** out to 24" x 8" (60 cm x 20 cm)

- **Fold again** ⅔ of the way to the other side and fold the other end in so that the two ends meet. Then in half like a book

- **This will give you** 16 layers of butter

- **Return the dough** to the fridge for another 30 minutes before repeating this process one more time

- **This will give you** a total of 64 layers

- **After this,** put the dough away in the fridge for the day

- **You can bake** the next day or up to 3 days later

DAY 3

SHAPE

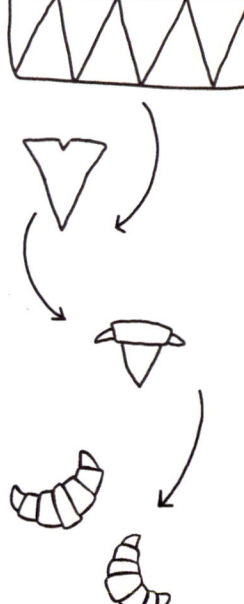

- **Flatten the same way** as before but roll the dough even longer than before: 43" (110 cm) long and 8" (20 cm) wide

- **Flour liberally** to prevent any breakage; you can brush off any excess before cutting

- **For crescent-shaped croissants,** on one long side, make a mark at every 5" (12.5 cm)

- **Along the other side,** make a mark at 2.5" (6.25 cm), then mark at every 5" (12.5 cm) after that

- **Now use a ruler's edge** and a sharp knife or pizza slicer to cut, joining the cut marks on either side to make triangles

- **One batch** can make 12 crescent shaped croissants

- **For the classic croissant shape,** gently stretch the bottom edge of the triangle making it a bit wider

- **Gently stretch** along the length as well

- **Roll up** as tightly as you can while handling the dough gently

- **Make sure the tip** of the tail ends up on the bottom so it stays tucked during baking

REST

- **Place the croissants** on parchment-lined baking sheets with about 2-3 inches of space between them
- **Keep in mind** they will double in size during this final rising plus more as they bake
- **Tent them** with plastic wrap to prevent a skin from forming on them as they rise
- **Use tall glasses** (or similar) to act as stands so the wrap doesn't touch the croissants
- **Let rise** in a warm location protected from drafts for 2 hours or until doubled in size
- **During the last 20 minutes,** preheat your oven to 400°F (205°C)

BAKE

- **Mix syrup wash** and gently brush on each croissant
- **Bake at 400°F** (205°C) for ten minutes
- **Then, lower the temperature** to 350°F (177°C)
- **Continue baking** for 20-25 minutes or until they are deep golden brown on top

FINISHING CROISSANTS

- **Rest croissants** on the baking sheets for 5 to 10 minutes before transferring to a cooking rack
- **Brush on a little bit more syrup** wash if before sprinkling any finishing salt or herbs

If you removed your croissants early (or if your oven runs a little cool) and found they weren't cooked all the way through after baking, don't worry! Just put them back in the hot oven at 350°F (177°C) for another 15 minutes or so. Keep an eye on them to prevent burning

Dogs and cats have always been incredibly important to me—I love them all. They taught me about the power of routines, from daily walks to meal times, their consistent presence grounding me each day. Despite their short lives, they bring such joy and teach me to cherish every moment, changing me forever. I learned early on that even a single thread of time spent with them is precious.

My companion Moleque, a rescue pug, taught me how to live in the present and have fun. His amazing personality and loyalty reminded me to enjoy life's simple pleasures. Whether barking at birds or lounging in the sun, he embraced each moment, especially when voicing his strong opinions on loud noises, uncomfortable beds, and food schedules.

As the years passed, I realized how time slips through our fingers. My first dog, Layka, passed away at 17 years old. Before my cats, Lisa and Pirate, passed at 18 years old each, they taught me the importance of enjoying every minute we have with each other. I introduced a new tradition into our home: celebrating their birthdays with parties and cakes.

I remember the first time Moleque, Lisa, and Pirate saw a peanut butter cake I bought. They eyed it skeptically, as if not believing it was meant for them. Moleque and Pirate ate the cake so fast, while Lisa preferred to smell its interesting scent. Since then, I've made it a tradition to bake their cakes myself.

I rescued another dog, Lime, and he's already obsessed with cakes. Dogs continue to teach me about love, resilience, and finding happiness in the small moments—whether it's a single dog treat or a birthday celebration—with cakes, of course.

I wanted to share this recipe here in case you'd like to embrace this tradition in your own homes. I joke that this recipe is diarrhea-free. As someone who strongly advocates for animal rights, I believe every animal deserves the world—and why not, the world with muffins!

BONUS: BLUEBERRY DOG MUFFINS!

Serving

Makes 6 medium-sized muffins

Timing

Bake for 25-30 minutes at 350°F (180°C)

Sugar Free

Nut Free

Ingredients

· 2 ripe bananas

· ⅓ cup (72 g) coconut oil

· ½ cup (125 ml) water

· 1 and ½ cups (195 g) unbleached flour

· 1 teaspoon (4 g) baking soda

· 1 tablespoon (15 ml) vinegar

· ⅓ cup (48 g) blueberries

Preparation

· **Preheat** the oven to 350°F (180°C)

· **Peel 2 bananas** and mash them until creamy

· **Mix the melted coconut oil** and water into the mashed bananas

· **Sift the unbleached flour** and baking soda into the banana mixture and mix well

· **Add the vinegar** to the batter and mix thoroughly

· **Gently fold** in the blueberries until evenly combined

· **Pour the batter** into the muffin cups

Freeze the blueberries before adding them to the recipe to make prettier muffins!

Finding happiness in the small moments—
whether it's a single dog treat or a birthday
celebration—with cakes, of course.

METRIC CHARTS

Cooking and especially baking can be challenging when recipes use unfamiliar measurement systems. Whether you're switching between metric and imperial units or need accurate measurements this guide has you covered.

Weight

Metric	Imperial
1 g	0.035 ounces
100 g	3.5 ounces (¼ pound)
200 g	7 ounces (½ pound)
500 g	17.6 ounces (1.1 pounds)
1,000 g (1 kg)	35 ounces (2.2 pounds)

Volume

Metric	Imperial
1 ml	0.034 fluid ounces
5 ml	1 teaspoon
15 ml	1 tablespoon
240 ml	1 cup
500 ml	2 cups (½ liter)
1,000 ml (1 L)	4 cups (1 quart)

Oven Temperatures

Metric	Imperial
100°C	212°F (boiling water)
160°C	325°F (low heat)
180°C	350°F (moderate heat)
200°C	400°F (hot oven)
220°C	425°F (very hot oven)

Common Conversions

Ingredient	Metric	Imperial
Flour	100 g	¾ cup
Sugar	200 g	1 cup
Butter	227 g	1 cup
Milk and Water	250 ml	1 cup

This book is a true labor of love, fueled by riot grrrl energy, *chingona* vibes, pug love, a do-it-yourself spirit, and the power of friendships.

When I told Izabelle at the beginning of 2024 that I would be celebrating a decade living in the United States in September, as well as a decade of being vegan, she immediately said, "Let's create a zine to celebrate." Just like that, everything started.

The zine quickly turned into a book. We got extra excited about everything! I initially wanted 10 recipes to celebrate 10 years, but then I decided to add an extra recipe to honor my dogs. The stories and recipes got longer. Maybe a zine will come later—who knows?

Looking back, I realized that I had been working on many of these recipes for years—*pão de queijo*, for instance, for a full decade. While other recipes came together more quickly, being able to veganize *pudim* brought me immense joy. It had been on my veganization list for quite some time, and accomplishing that felt like a triumph.

A special thanks goes to my partner, Koji, who has always encouraged me. I think he's never eaten as many cakes, *pudins, brigadeiros*, crème brûlées, cookies, *pães de queijo*, and pies in his entire life! I'm sure he had mixed feelings—loving the treats but finding it hard to stop eating them—while I was surprisingly showing more self-control. Koji's support was essential in making this book possible, and a special shoutout for the cool croissant illustrations!

This book wouldn't have been possible without the support of my community and friends, who continuously encouraged me with their kind words and constructive feedback. Trying different iterations of the recipes takes courage, and I recognize that giving honest feedback can be challenging. I always invited my friends to share their thoughts openly: "Please tell me the truth. We're in a safe space, and I need to know how to improve."

Another special shoutout goes to the Vegan Lanches community—"*lanches*" means snacks in Portuguese—our Vegan Snacks group, made up of Brazilian friends living in the Bay Area. We support each other and are always planning food adventures. Thank you to Christine, Cíntia, Júlia, Juliana Almeida, Koji, Marina Tai, Tiago, and Yuri for your support, enthusiasm while trying my recipes, and all these years of friendship.

I want to thank Amanda, Bene, Clara, Clayton, Danielle, Faisal, Fernanda, Flávia, Giles, Jennifer, Juliana Cogo, Juliana Lima, Letícia, Lígia, Lucas, Marianne Abreu, Navneet, Olivia, Patrícia Albanese, Patrícia Queiroz, Rafael, Ri, Rohan, Saab, Senna, Xande, and my neighbors, who gladly tested my recipes and shared valuable feedback.

Lastly, a big thank you to my family and friends cheering me on from afar: Ana Cimbleris, Ana Júlia, Juliana Gallo, Anderson, Camila, Carlos, Clarissa Lage, Clarissa Quetz, Felipe, Francisco, Fred, Guilherme, Linete, Ludmila, Marina Jordá-Poblet, Renata, Sayonara, Sillas, and Vanessa.

Years ago, I heard this quote: "If you want to go fast, go alone; if you want to go far, go together." It has always stuck with me. I've worked on personal projects for a long time, usually alone, and I often thought it would be great to collaborate with someone who could complement my skills. That's exactly what happened with Izabelle. Her ideas and get-it-done attitude always inspired me. Before our photoshoots, I would often message her, worried that the recipe wouldn't turn out as expected or be pretty enough for the pictures. Izabelle always understood my concerns and helped me push through. This book wouldn't have turned out the way it did without her. You're an essential part of this project, Iza. Obrigada.

A shout out to our partners, Koji and Izabelle's partner, Benjamim, who served as hand models and also helped us prepare the scenarios and photo shoots—especially when the photo shoot involved two hungry pugs who happen to love eating anything!

Talking about dogs, Lime and Moleque were essential "helpers" during the development of this book. They were always attentively watching and giving me support while I cooked countless times, which also caused some trouble—every time I bake something now, they think I'm making them blueberry dog muffins!

Thank you to all my friends, family, and community who believe in my work and continue to support me.

Obrigada!
Thaisa Fernandes

I dedicate this book to my son, Jorge Salim, who decided to join our lives two months into this project and has been growing inside me alongside it ever since. I am so proud to be baking a book *and* a baby at the same time. I hope you'll one day look back and feel good about this journey. You were there with us, all the time.

I've always dreamed of working on a cookbook project. So, when Thaisa told me she was celebrating 10 years of being vegan and living in the U.S., I knew this was one of those moments you just can't let slip by.

At the time, I was deeply immersed in my project, Visual Food Journal, taking photos of my favorite subject, food. So it was very natural to propose to her to create a recipe zine together! The fusion of these passions sparked the idea for the book you're now holding.

As a team, we set out to transform Thaisa's stories into visual narratives filled with warmth and joy. I started sketching concepts (you can spot some on the final pages) while Thaisa tested her recipes tirelessly, over and over. This stage of the project was pure fun—and incredibly tasty!

Once the recipes were perfected, we scheduled shoot dates, and I pulled together props for each photo from items I had at home or found at a nearby art store. Back then, the project was still envisioned as a zine, so we decided I'd shoot everything with my Pixel phone. Hiring a photographer wasn't an option, and we didn't want to wait, so we thought, sure, why not?!

Even though I've been working for years as a professional graphic designer and art director, I'm not a professional photographer. What you see here is the result of a lot of DIY spirit, curiosity, and pure love for the process.

I'm sharing this because I want people to know that creating a book doesn't require perfection or endless resources. What you really need is commitment, passion, organization

(and I must say, we are both pretty good at it!), great food, and some clotheslines for hanging backdrops (think bedsheets, rugs, and anything you can repurpose!).

That being said, I want to thank my partner, Benjamim, for his endless patience throughout the shoots, for always being by my side, and for stepping in as a hand model whenever needed. Your kindness and encouragement mean the world to me.

I'm also deeply grateful for the incredible Bay Area community, whose support helped make this book possible. From production help and modeling to recipe feedback and text suggestions, thank you. A special shoutout to Koji, Thaisa's partner, for capturing behind-the-scenes moments while we were lost in caramels, doughs, and velvets.

Finally, to Thaisa: thank you for your partnership, dedication, and contagious positivity. Working with you was an absolute joy, and I'm so proud of what we created together. Your delicious recipes are inspiring, and I love that this project brought us together and turned into a real friendship.

Muito obrigada!
Izabelle Alvares

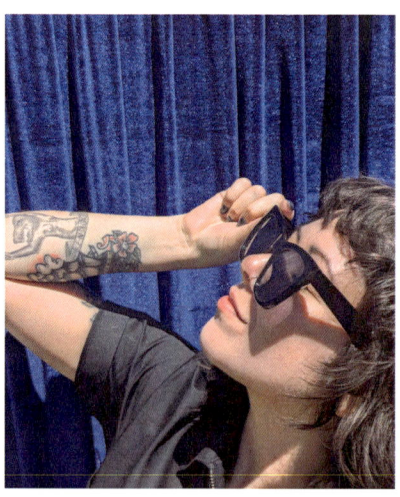

58

THE
PROCESS

A peek on what the last 8 months looked liked for us. Consider this as a sign if you're thinking of starting a new project and don't know where to begin. Do it yourself and have fun!

PÃO DE QUEIJO (CHEESE BREAD)

Tons of *pães de queijo*, in many different flavors, I don't know about you but it feels like heaven to me.

BRAZILIAN CARROT CAKE

Iza had food poisoning that day but we still managed to shoot under the sun. Talk about commitment!

GOIABINHA
(GUAVA COOKIE)

PUDIM (BRAZILIAN FLAN)

We quickly learned that for the style we wanted, a hard natural light would be the best way to shoot. The weather was very nice and we always tried to shoot during the afternoon, when the sun was up so we would have lighting consistency.

BRIGADEIRO (CHOCOLATE TRUFFLE)

PISTACHIO + CHOCOLATE COOKIE

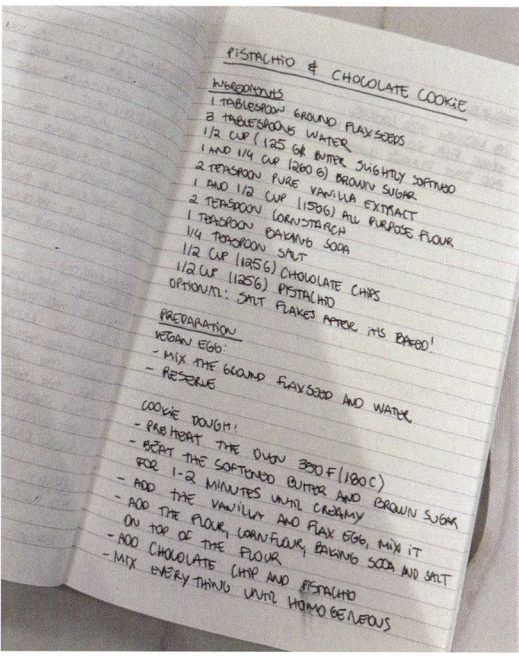

PISTACHIO & CHOCOLATE COOKIE

INGREDIENTS
1 TABLESPOON GROUND FLAXSEEDS
3 TABLESPOONS WATER
1/2 CUP (125 GR) BUTTER SLIGHTLY SOFTENED
1 AND 1/4 CUP (280 G) BROWN SUGAR
2 TEASPOON PURE VANILLA EXTRACT
1 AND 1/2 CUP (150G) ALL PURPOSE FLOUR
2 TEASPOON CORNSTARCH
1 TEASPOON BAKING SODA
1/4 TEASPOON SALT
1/2 CUP (125G) CHOCOLATE CHIPS
1/2 CUP (125G) PISTACHIO
OPTIONAL: SALT FLAKES AFTER ITS BAKED!

PREPARATION
VEGAN EGG:
- MIX THE GROUND FLAXSEED AND WATER
- RESERVE

COOKIE DOUGH:
- PRE HEAT THE OVEN 350 F (180 C)
- BEAT THE SOFTENED BUTTER AND BROWN SUGAR
  FOR 1-2 MINUTES UNTIL CREAMY
- ADD THE VANILLA AND FLAX EGG, MIX IT
- ADD THE FLOUR, CORN FLOUR, BAKING SODA AND SALT
  ON TOP OF THE FLOUR
- ADD CHOCOLATE CHIP AND PISTACHIO
- MIX EVERYTHING UNTIL HOMOGENEOUS

VANILLA CAKE

That was our first shot, the only one indoors and we had a lot of learnings from it.

SWEET POTATO PIE

A few oranges were burnt in the process.

CREME BRULÉE

It took us some time, but we figured out how to make caramel look like broken glass pieces.

CROISSANT

Everything gets better when we have friends supporting us and anxiously waiting the moment they could eat the croissants.

BONUS: BLUEBERRY DOG MUFFINS!

Lime got so excited about the muffins that he jumped and tore the backyard furniture!

SKETCHES

Here you can see some of the skecthes I started with. They might not look great, but you gotta start somewhere, right? These ensured all images would look good and cohesive amongst each other and were a life saver for the styling process.

www.ingramcontent.com/pod-product-compliance
Lightning Source LLC
Chambersburg PA
CBRC090843120626
46551CB00009B/744